My Heart Is Yours

Poetry by Ajanay

Ajanay Bonner

BookLeaf
Publishing
India | USA | UK

Made with ❤ on the BookLeaf Publishing Platform

www.bookleafpub.in

www.bookleafpub.com

Dedication

To the souls once shattered by love's loss,
lift your eyes — your story isn't done.
With God, even ashes bloom,
and every loss becomes a win.
Welcome to your winning season!

Preface

What is love?

Through life we go through seasons where, sadly, we learn what love is NOT. We think we know what love is based on movies, social media and our own fantasies. We burn ourselves out chasing this false romanticized "love" that is truly LUST. Only after suffering through the pain of what love is not, have I decided to dive deep into what LOVE really is. I know that God provides us with the purest form of love. So I am deciding to de-program myself of everything society has brainwashed me into believing what love is; and I am taking on God's definition of love. I want to love with purity of heart. I want to love the way Christ loves us. With this type of love I know I will be a light in this world. Hopefully with my transformation in love will I inspire others to love, so they may become a brighter light themselves.

"Love suffers long *and* is kind; love does not envy; love does not parade itself, is not puffed up; does not behave rudely, does not seek its own, is not provoked, thinks no evil; does not rejoice in iniquity, but rejoices in the truth; bears all things, believes all things, hopes all things, endures all things. Love never fails..." -1 Corinthians 13:4-8 NKJV

Acknowledgements

This book would not be possible without the inspiration and guidance of my heavenly Father through Jesus Christ my Lord and savior. He has personally instilled in me the courage and mental fortitude to pursue the desires placed in my heart. So thank you God for the many gifts you have put in me. I hope these gifts are received well by those blessed to experience them.
Amen.

"Trust in the Lord with all your heart,
And lean not on your own understanding;
In all your ways acknowledge Him,
And He shall direct your paths." -Proverbs 3:5-6

1. Siren

Your beauty is beyond measure, beyond words.
To describe the wonder of your light is to explain colors
to the blind
Your very essence is divine

By nature you are good.

So good for me that I can not bear it.
Your love is a mesmerizing ocean of soothing waves that
sways me gently into peace.
The lulling waves surround me and I feel one with the
sea of our passion.
Floating in your deep waters
Surrounded by your love to no end.

But yet I thirst...

I drink in your devotion and adoration
but yet I thirst for more.

You continue to pour into me.
I consume your love offering until my belly is full of salt
and my bones are brittle and my essence dry...

The infinite beauty that is you.
So pleasing to the eye, dazzling to my senses
But my body can not sustain to remain in your love.

So deep and blue and mystical
I mourn to run away from your love.
But to stay in it is to dry out or drown..

I swim away to shore
Your current pulls me back in and I'm floating,
But my peace is gone.

I swim harder to get away.
A riptide draws me in deeper than before.
I try to float but the waves are crashing over my head

I am afraid.

The waves that were once my fantasy
Are now the means to my end.
Drowning in your deep
Frantically praying for a savior

I close my eyes
And I hold my breath.

I open my eyes to find I am standing on the shore.

Toes in the sand, as small waves splash my feet.
I take a deep breath as I gaze upon the beauty of the sea.

Enchanted once again.

Like a moth to a burning flame,
I walk deeper and deeper
Back in.

2. ...and man became a living soul

Out of the dust was I made and back to dust shall I
return
What could I ever do to earn
a love so great and true
That The Holy One would find me worthy
to receive the spirit of the truth
Who am I to think myself divine,
for I know where I am from.
Yet my God
He calls me Chosen
for I was made NEW through HIS SON.
My God MY God has not forsaken me
for prophecy is fulfilled
The only begotten of the father
Rose from the dead After He was killed
His body was bruised and broken
so that mine now shall be healed.
I ask The Father for His Holy Spirit
and now, Glory be to God, I am Filled.

Greatness dwells within me.

3. Petals and Thorns

Just as flowers grow in the spring time
My feelings for you are beginning to bloom
like roses
so beautiful and enticing

but I shouldn't be so inviting

because just like bushes of roses,
untamed feelings have thorns.

A small prick of a finger is not fatal,
but a prick to the heart can feel just as deadly as a sword.

4. Thoughts

Still thinking about you
can't get you out of my mind
feel like I'm losing my mind
I'm losing the time

It's only been a few days
Feels like a life time
When you look in my eyes

Cant believe that's your mind
I wish you were mine
When I met you I knew this love was a one of a kind

I hope I never forget you
But my spirit will never forget

That I gave it my all
so I will never regret.

5. Dead Flowers

She said she fell in a rose bush
as she pulled down her sleeve.

I've never seen an accidental fall leave markings so clean.

She said that it was nothing
as she pulled her arm away.

I always wished I would have did more.
I still think of her to this day.

Dead flowers don't smell the same
Their beauty and colors fade away.

You try to save them anyway you know how
but somehow they still decay.

There's nothing you can do
but accept the ugly truth,

that you were just a little too late.

6. I'm over it

Why do you only call me to ignore my calls?
why do you always say you love me to ignore my love?

The more I get set free the more you fight for me
and when I finally give in
you push me away again.

Please don't confuse me.
Please don't use me.

I am tired of being drained from playing your little game.

I'm too amazing
I'm too tough
to keep giving into you
just for you to say that I'm too much.

Well, I call your bluff.

I'm over it.

7. I can't love you if I don't love myself

She's so pretty, she's so witty
I really really like her.
Her smile makes me weak
The laughter that she brings, I think about her all dang week.
I just want her to myself.
I want to make her mine.
But when ever I get the chance I just seem to lose my mind.

Why do I sabotage myself?
I know what I want but I feel I'm undeserving.
Why do I do it to myself?
She finally gave me the chance
and I let her slip right through my hands.

Maybe I don't want to be happy.
Because when I'm happy it makes me scared.
Maybe I don't want to be happy because
what if
happiness doesn't last the way I dreamed it would.
Maybe I don't deserve to be happy.
Misery is my familiar company.

I don't know how to be happy.

So I'll just push her away again before she walks away
from me.
I'm addicted to the pain of being alone
Because the pain of being left is far more scary.
I'd rather leave than lose her again.
I'm okay with pain. I'll just walk away.

But, what if I want to be happy....

Well, now she's moving on.
Am I too late?

Baby please you're the only one that makes me happy...

She said she's over it.

I guess I'll go back to what I know...
My own self hate.

8. Deception

One day man wished upon a STAR

The star fell so close he thought it was God.

The star granted wishes and made dreams come TRUE

Man was dumfounded and tricked with no clue.

The star would give in order to take.

The man would keep wishing not knowing the stakes.

The star gave man the WORLD and ancient knowledge of old

But man was not wise to see he has lost his eternal soul.

9. Chosen

I'm so in love with you
I feel like it's a dream.
What do you mean I'm the one you chose?
Me?
I push you away because It's hard to believe
someone like you would ever love me.
But time and time and time again
you show me a love deeper and older than when time
began

You showed me my purpose.

My purpose to shine and be a light that burns greater
everyday.
The past told me to dim
but you have shown me a better way.

10. Stay

The truth?
You want the truth?
The truth is...
I don't know how to trust.
I say I trust you everyday but I guess you've called my
bluff.
I want you
but sometimes I just don't want to change.
The cost of loving you
is that I can not stay the same.
I love you no doubt,
but if you loved me the way I've been loving you
I don't think we would have made it this far.
I'm sorry.
Have I been deceived?
I don't ever want to be away from you
help me God please.
Teach me how to love you.
Teach me your ways.
You are my first love
I've left you behind
but you have Never left me.
You're with me
always,

stay
with
me.

11. Someone special

Pretty eyes, sparkling smile,
but thats not what has my heart beating like I just ran a
thousand miles.
It's your mind, it's your intellect.
It's the way you're saying what I am thinking,
and thinking what I say.
Each conversation makes me glad you came to talk
when we met the other day.
You don't just remind me of me
but you remind me of everything God told me I'm
supposed to be.
Sprung is not the word.
You got me singing an inner song and I can't make out
the words.
Your light is so beautiful.
I really can't get enough.
You motivate me to be better.
You're a real go getter, goal setter, Gold getter.
I like that.
You can teach me things I never knew.
You already got me smiling and blushing and doing
things I never do.
Who are you?
I want to know you more.

12. Unstable in all your ways

I know what my name is
But I don't know who I am.
I know what I've been through
But I don't know who's I am.
I know where I come from I know where I've been
I know the things I've done and seen
But I don't know where I belong.
I know my thoughts and my desires
But I have no idea
who I am.
Who am I?
Why am I like this?
Why am I this way?
I don't want to be this way anymore.
I say it so often but it never changes.
Why is that?
I don't get it.
I don't understand,
the more I want to change
the more I start to do things the same
and it doesn't make any sense.
I try to dig my self out but I only make the hole deeper
and deeper.

I'm buried alive I can't breath I don't know what's going to happen next.

I'm clearly failing at this test

because I don't know the answers.

The answers are not conventional.

These riddles get more confusing the more you try to answer them.

So don't answer them.

Don't even try.

Every possible answer is a lie.

You're a lie.

Who's a lie? Who me?

You don't even know me.

Everything you do is in an attempt to destroy me.

You can't control me.

You think you own me?

You don't so don't act like you do.

Where's the respect I deserve the respect I am due.

What is your problem?

How about you make up your mind and decide who you want to follow.

13. Faith is the substance

I feel inadequate
Unprepared
Under qualified
Who am I to do the impossible?
Who am I to beat the odds?
Doing things that have never been done
I hold on to the saying "it's already been won!"
God showed me the promise
He said it must be fulfilled

He said "don't you know
that I'm the Father that owns the cattle upon a thousand
hills.
In due time you will see.
you shall become everything I have designed you to be."

14. Toxic Lover

I know you love me...
but why do you wait till my face is stained with tears
to tell me how you feel?
That makes my mind spin so bad
even my body can't be still...
Are you using these words to manipulate me
the way you know they will?
I'm scared of you.
Worried if your love is fake
and even more terrified that it's real...
I want to trust the words you say
and one day for sure I will...
but the thought
that this is just a game you play
runs up my spine with chills...
Aches of a broken heart are strong enough to kill...
so do you mean what you say?
Or am I another victim who's fallen for your wicked
skill....
Heartache is the price to pay
when a heart of gold can't pay the bill.

15. Rose Tinted Glasses

Living in a fantasy
The birds are singing as the Sun rays light up the room
The romantic smell of roses fill the air when I think of
you
My darling you
Your smile makes me feel like I am floating on a cloud
Our love abounds
Staring into each other's eyes
We get lost in the sea of love that is us
So much love and so much trust
Our feelings so deep and strong
I sleep in peace knowing you will never do me wrong
You would never hurt my heart
You've been loyal since the start
You love me
I'm a princess in your eyes
and you are my King
You take care of me
My best friend
My everything
You are Mr. Perfect
In my fantasy

Living in reality

You are the one
That broke my heart
You've been playing me from the start
How could you?!
The villain to my love story
The one who betrayed my love
You did me so wrong
You lie in my face and stab me in the back
You were supposed have my back
Sleepless nights thinking of how you hurt me
How could you desert me?
Do you hate me?
The thought of you with her is so heavy my chest caves
in
My mind fills with despair as I remember what used to
be
My silent sobs in the dark
Leave your pillow soaked in my pain
In my reality

16. Caught In A Trance

I am not amused
With the constant pandering of propaganda

The media never stops
Social media never locks

It keeps flooding out stories and posts
And I can't stop

I keep taking it in
Locked in a scrolling whirlwind
I look up

And I can't remember how I got this far gone
This is not fun anymore

I want to keep writing how I feel but
I was locked out of my mind for so long,
I don't know what's in it
I've been on auto pilot for a little minute

I am looking for my muse
It's been lost for a little while.

I want my imagination to become free
Like back when I was a little child

I have to unplug
So my spirit can be charged up

Disconnect from the matrix
Bring myself back to earth

Stop following Man
And start putting God first

17. Invisible

If I were invisible
I guess I'd feel the same way I do right now
I mean.. I am invisible
Nobody truly sees me for who I am
I don't feel visible
Feel like I'm stuck in the lost & found
But nobody's looking for me

I mean yes it's messed up..the way it sounds
But I guess that's just how
it's supposed to be
I've seen a lot of things go south
That's why it's so hard to let people get close to me
All my past friendships and loves
They're nothing now but ghosts to me

A haunting remembrance
Of all the things I've given
All the things they've taken
Yes my heart still aching
I'm always bending backwards
Now my back is breaking

I've had enough it's too much

I had to cut it out
I had to cut em off

But just because they're gone
Doesn't mean the problems solved
It's time to evolve

And it's not that I want to be seen
I want to be heard

I'm tired of being last
Tired of being second
And third
I am second to none
I am a child of God
It's time to put me first
I'm done

18. Feeling low

Sometimes...
I just want to die
And it's hard for me to understand why.
I think of all the things I'm blessed to have
And everything I'm thankful for.
I think of all my friends and family
All those whom I adore.
Yet for some reason late at night
When I close my eyes and with all my might,
Try to just get some rest.
All I can think of is my death.
I hate to sound so dark and morbid.
I hate to think that I'm depressed.
But when I think about my thoughts
I realize my mind is just a mess
But could it be just a test
To see if I'll last
for the rest...

of this life and its plans

19. Redefining

Love is a verb..
So don't tell me that you love me
If all your actions lead to hurt
Love is something you do
Not just a thing you say in an attempt to make me stay
It's not just a word you throw out to make everything
okay
Love is being patient when we don't see eye to eye
Love is forgiving each other and not dwelling in our
strife
Love is unconditional
Kindness during a fight
Telling the truth when it would be easier to lie
Just being there to show you care
Apologizing for pain you've caused while unaware
When I say I love you I'm saying I won't judge you
I'm saying that I'll trust you even though I've been hurt
before
I'm saying I will be here for you when it seems you have
no one else
I'm saying that I care about your needs as much as I care
about my self
Actions speak louder than words
So let your actions scream your love into the heavens

let your love be seen before it's heard
And if that seems impossible... too big a task to ask...
It's likely that your ego feels attacked
In which case I hope one day your pride will move aside
And allow you to know real love
Proper and true
Love is a verb
It's not something you say
It's something we do .... ❤

20. Waning Crescent

Just as the moon has different phases
I have different faces
That I show dependent on different cases
But I noticed no matter what phase I'm in
When I'm with you my mind races
Trying to figure out how you could put up with me
despite my many changes
My trust
It ranges
From little to none but you some how change this
You make the truths that have been locked up inside of
me come out of its cages
It's just so hard to speak it
If I had to write it all down the world could not provide
enough pages
But I can say this
Thank you for being you and allowing me to be me
Thank you for understanding and for helping me to see
That I'm not alone and there's people that really care
I'm very grateful for all the time, truth, fun, love, and
moments that we share.
So just so you know
No matter what phase I'm in

Forever in my heart
You will always be my friend.

21. Self Reflecting

You've shown me myself
And I don't like what I see
All the ugly things I picked out in others... were really in
me
I've turned into a person I never wanted to be
I thought doing whatever I wanted meant I was free
But how am I free if I'm not being me
I finally see
It's my own ego that's been my enemy

22. Liars never change

Anger fills my blood

As I lay awake thinking about what you've put me through...
the lies you spake directly to my face
how could your tongue allow it?
The same mouth that betrayed me
Now begs my forgiveness with promises to be different?
Would I be a fool to believe it?
Is it possible for you to really change...
Only moments after you've seen my pain?
Or is it that my pain makes you see exactly who you are
that you are exactly the thing you don't want to be?
The tears on my face reflecting back to you your own disgrace.
You see the hurt in my eyes, you hear it in my voice...
you say you're sorry, but your sorry doesn't change your choice.
In life we have choices, and you made the wrong one.
Why am I the one to suffer because YOU wanted to have "fun".
Now I lay awake with inner turmoil because I can't decide
Whether being with you or leaving you would be a faster suicide...

23. Message from my higher self

You've really changed...
and to be honest lately you've been acting kind of
strange...
it's like I don't even know you any more
or like you don't know me....
But I mean how could it be...
it's like.. you're forgetting all about me...
you made promises to me
and you're breaking every last one.
It's like you enjoy hurting me.
Ruining my heart just for fun...
I use to be your number one..
remember?
No of course you don't. Now to you I'm just a joke.
You treat me like a toy and for what?
This world that destroys!
You're just trying to fill the void.
You're not happy
I can hear it in your voice.
I can see it in your eyes.
I can tell by that fake smile..
You don't even laugh the same...
you're not even half the same.

I can't even articulate half the shame
That I feel when you try to explain
and over compensate for the things you've done
in the name of fun.

24. A New Creation

I've been changing into someone new
Changing into someone who
Doesn't tolerate the things
that I always used to do

I used to try to please everyone else
I put everyone's needs before my self

I used to spread myself so thin
Questioned if I'd ever win
Got so bound up in my sin

I had to die to myself in order to truly live.
The old me is gone.
The new is taking root.
I'm completely different now
living in the truth.

25. Soulless

I don't want you to like me
I don't want you to want me
I want you to use me and abuse me
Because wether you do right by me or not
You're still going to lose me
That's why I'm saying
Don't choose me
Choose yourself
I can already tell
I'm not good for your health
I bring people emotional hell
I'm emotionless... hell
Don't stick with me you'll be motionless
never moving, stagnant, stuck
I don't want your love
I just want to f>ck
But
I don't want to f>ck
Up
Your heart
You're too good for that
Don't pretend like you can handle it
Thinking you're "too hood" for that
Im like an evil siren

My voice and beauty draws you in
Makes you let your guard down
Then my shenanigans begin
Leading you to a horrible fate
With you never realizing until it's too late
I'm everything you like and more
I make it easy for you to open up your doors
You think I'm sweet and easy to adore
But I'm not I'm fucked up in the head
We really messed up when we laid in that bed
I feel so guilty thinking of the tears you'll shed
But at the same time when I'm alone I feel dead
And the day i'll have to leave you alone I still dread
I'm sorry I don't know why I'm like this
so many things I wish I never said

26. Tell me the Truth

Tell me the truth...
Am I just but flesh to you
Do you only want me if I'm naked laying next to you?
Do you have any a concern about my soul?
Or is getting in my pants your only goal?
It's clear that you don't even care about my feelings.
Your actions tell me more than what your words are
revealing.

And I suppose it's time that I stop concealing
and I guess start dealing with how I am feeling
Because this pain is really killing...
Me softly gently and sweetly
the same way you came and swept me off my feet.
Your smile deceivingly true and pure
for all of my sadness you were the only cure.
never knowing that I would soon endure
the savagely inhuman torture on my heart.
A terrible truth that tore me apart.
Something I should have seen from the very start.

When you first said you loved me and I melted.
It's then when I should have felt it.
It's then when I should have known

that this false paradise would not last too long.

The day when we first kissed.

A day I once had missed is now a day I that makes me hiss.

A huge ping of regret that travels from my head and through my chest.

How could I have been so blind.

I should have never made you mine.

You killed me

you destroyed me

you ruined my life.

The pain you caused me deadlier than a knife

you did not care.

But yet you never dared..

To just tell me the truth.

27. Forever Changed

Depression is like a ball and chain weighted to my ankle
Pulling me down so deep I can't see where I even am
anymore
Who I am anymore
How did I get here?

How to resurface
out of this dark furnace
Of self hatred and self destruction
I pray to God for one ounce of a clue to his instructions

Why must I be this way?
The answer so clear but yet
doesn't seem very near

I'm in the desert wandering in my depression
So thirsty for the resurrection
of my soul
I've been so dead
Speak to these dry bones
Wake me up out of this despair
I need you here
I need you here
Reach out and touch me God

you spoke the world into existence
Lord remake my world in this one instance

you have the keys to my new start

you've changed everything for me
And once I surrendered
you gave me a new heart

the chains are broken now
for there is liberty in Christ

I am a living testimony
of God bringing a dead man back to life
so I will sing His praises
all the days that I am given
Because it is Only by HIS grace and mercy that
I am still here amongst the living
GLORY TO GOD!
Amen.

28. BONUS

Silent Screams

Can't lie
it's hard not to cry
you spread yourself so thin
to seem happy you have to lie
to be happy you have to hide
not just hide from the world
but hide from your friends
hide from your family and nobody understands
you're only human and you have feelings too
It's time for you to know that there's nothing you have to
prove
being true to you will never make you lose
the only time you lose is when you end up losing you
when you end up losing truth
then you end up losing faith
and your heart get filled with hate
and your soul just starts to ache
you realize it's time
time for you to awake

It's crazy how living out your dream can turn into a
nightmare
and I'm only being real in the hopes that I might scare

myself
back into reality
tired of living a fallacy
tired of living in vain
tired of letting my soul have to suffer in so much pain
fighting to be heard and wanting to be seen
trying to show the world what being me really means
it's much deeper than it seems
I wish people could read my mind so they could hear my
silent screams